EDWARD LAROCQUE TINKER

CORRIDOS & CALAVERAS

With notes and translations by Americo Paredes
THE UNIVERSITY OF TEXAS

Published by
HUMANITIES RESEARCH CENTER
THE UNIVERSITY OF TEXAS, AUSTIN
Distributed by the
UNIVERSITY OF TEXAS PRESS

Library of Congress Catalog Card Number 61–63839

Made in The United States of America

CORRIDOS & CALAVERAS

EVERY IBERO-AMERICAN LOVES
POETRY AND THERE IS HARDLY A
LITERATE MAN AMONG THEM WHO HAS NOT
AT SOME TIME WRITTEN VERSE. THE EX-
tent of their passionate addiction is amusingly illustrated by a hap-
pening during the Mexican Revolution. A body of *Federales* had
defeated a band of *Revolucionarios* and were hunting down the
fugitives. Finding a man hidden in the branches of a tree, they were
about to shoot him when he yelled, 'Don't! don't! I'll come down.
I'm a poet!'

Immediately guns were grounded, and the *cancionero* climbed
down and spent the night, safe and happy, singing his *corridos*
around the campfire to the delight of his captors.

I shall never forget the first time I heard one of these songs of
the people.

I had been living in El Paso installing a 'Safety First' organi-
zation for a railroad. The Mexican Revolution was in its bloody
apogee and this border town swarmed with blacklegs, gun-runners,
refugees, and soldiers of fortune. United States cavalry guarded
the frontier, and General Pershing was in command at Fort Bliss.

5

Rumors were rife of battles and massacres below the border and there was a feeling of tenseness and excitement throughout the city. No day passed that one couldn't have stumbled on a typical 'O. Henry' story.

At that time our State Department was uncertain as to which side to recognize, so it had sent representatives to both. George Carrothers was the special agent to Pancho Villa, and meeting him in the street, I invited him into the Paso del Norte for a drink. He was a heavily built man with a round, impassive, poker face and a tummy that polite Mexicans would have described as having 'the curve of felicity'; and he knew Latino psychology as a cow knows its calf.

As we sipped our drinks, I asked what was going on below the border, and he answered: 'Villa is in Juarez and he's raised the biggest army Mexico has ever seen, and he's going down to Celaya to lock horns with General Alvaro Obregón. I'm going with him,' and then as an afterthought he asked: 'Do you want to come along?'

'Tarantulas', I shot back, 'and rattlesnakes couldn't stop me.'

The trip in Villa's troop train was an unbelievable saga I shall never forget, but that is for some other telling.

The army finally detrained a few miles north of Celaya, which Obregón had surrounded with well placed trenches and fortifications, and after some days wait, the attack began.

One of Villa's most trusted generals was Manuel Banda, a man of the most reckless daring, who had been a dishwasher in a third-rate Chicago hotel and had returned to his native land to join the army. On the day of the first assault, he saw that two cannons on the roof of a house in Celaya, near where the railroad entered town, were doing a deal of damage to his forces.

At the head of his troop train was a flat car on which was mounted a heavy cannon, affectionately known as 'El Niño' (the Boy), and the locomotive came next. Uncoupling the back cars, Banda, an expert engineer, jumped into the cab, pulled the whistle cord, and headed his tiny train straight for Celaya, with the throttle wide open.

Seeing this, the enemy gunners fired on the approaching cars, but missed again and again, and each time Banda celebrated by a derisive whistle-toot. When he got into the outskirts, he opened fire with 'El Niño' and put the enemy cannons out of business.

Obregón reinforcements began to come up, and Banda, having accomplished his mission, threw his engine in reverse and high-tailed it safely back to Villa's lines.

The night after this exploit, as I wandered along the boxcars on which the troops were quartered on the roofs, I heard singing and the strumming of stringed instruments. Following my ears I came into the light of a campfire around which a crowd of Villa's ragged soldiers were gathered with their *soldaderas*—those amazing Amazons who cooked for their men and, with pots and pans, and often a baby on their backs, kept up with the regiment on gruelling marches; or, when need arose, snatched a rifle from a corpse and fought as fiercely as any male. This strange motley crowd, most of them showing strong strains of Aztec, was listening in the moon-light like fascinated children to the singing of three men. One was a thin, hatchet-faced mestizo with the sly look of a coyote, another a young Indio with the rapt expression of a choir boy; while, between the two, twanging a guitar, was a man in a dirty yellow charro suit. He had a harelip and a gross torso that looked like a huge Easter egg propped up on match sticks—the ugliest human being I ever saw.

As I listened to the assonances of their voices, I too was fasci-nated, and thought they sang some old folk tale. As verse after verse, however, took the same melodic pattern, I suddenly realized that this was no ancient epic, but a fresh-minted account of the battle of the day before, because it described in detail Banda's heroic action. It was a *corrido*—hot from the oven of their vivid memory of the struggle between Villa and Obregón—the first one I had ever heard.

But it was not until the Carnegie Endowment for International Peace sent me to Mexico in 1943 to lecture at the National Uni-versity on North American idealistic literature that I got a chance to study the subject and came to realize that these *cancioneros*, like the *payadores* of Argentina and Uruguay, were, in almost every essential, the lineal descendants of the troubadors who performed at the Court of Eleanore of Aquitaine in the middle of the 12th century, and that their songs were the Creole counterpart of the early Spanish *romances*, those Iberian *chansons de geste* in which countless mediaeval bards sang the fabulous exploits of Hispanic knights to the accompaniment of the *lira mendicoram*—*romances*

7

which must have come to America with the Conquistadores, for Bernal Díaz wrote that one of Cortez' soldiers, named Ortiz, was a *tocador de bihuela* (a guitar-like instrument of Moorish design) and taught dancing.

In colonial days, because of the dominance of the church, the early songs had a distinctly moralistic cast, and celebrated saints, or related miracles. But as time went on, they became secular, sometimes even scurrilous, so the horrified Holy Tribunal of the Mexican Inquisition denounced them for 'scandalously *running* through the city.' One authority, Evans Clark, argues that the broad-sheet ballads owe their name to this incident, and were called *corridos* because of it. Another scholar, Vicente Mendoza, suggests it was because the melody ran or flowed so easily and gaily; but the vulgar explanation is that some of the verses were so libellous that the

'LOS 41 MARICONES'

This *corrido*, the product of a scandal occurring during the Porfirio Díaz regime, gave to Mexican folk speech the term 'cuarenta y uno' (forty- one), meaning "homosexual.' On November 20, 1901, police raided a formal ball at La Paz street and arrested forty-one young men belonging to Mexico City's fashionable society. Half the young men were found in white tie and tails, the other half in evening gowns. Some of the 'ladies' were carrying dolls.

It is said that Porfirio Díaz himself took a hand in the matter. After a night in jail the young men in male attire went to the barracks of the mounted police to clean the stables. Those in women's clothes were set to sweeping the streets. The plebeians of the capital, who had no great love for the Díaz aristocracy, hugely enjoyed the spectacle. The 'forty-one' then were drafted into the army (a common punishment for all sorts of wrongdoing in Díaz' time); and they were sent to Yucatán, where the Maya Indians were in rebellion at the time.

Newspaper accounts in this instance were the source of the Vanegas Arroyo broadsides, the one reproduced here being one of several. It was not the newspaper stories, however, but the broadsides which reached the people and made a deeply lasting impression. Posada's prints, illustrating the scurrilous details of the *corrido* verses with a fidelity greater than life, had much to do with the permanent effect of the broadsides on the minds of Mexicans everywhere. Sixty years after the *maricones* staged their ball on La Paz street, Texas-Mexicans use 'forty-one'—in English—to mean 'homosexual,' though perhaps not one in a thousand knows the origin of the term.

8

1 : *Translation on page 42*

LOS 41 MARICONES

Encontrados en un baile de la Calle de la Paz el 20 de Noviembre de 1901

Aquí están los Maricones

MUY CHULOS Y COQUETONES

Hace aún muy pocos días
Que en la calle de la Paz,
Los gendarmes atisbaron
Un gran baile singular.

Cuarenta y un lagartijos
Disfrazádos la mitad
De simpáticas muchachas
Bailaban como el que más.

La otra mitad con su traje,
Es decir de masculinos,
Gozaban al extrechar
A los *famosos jotitos*.

Vestidos de raso y seda
Al último figurín,
Còn pelucas bien peinadas
Y moviéndose con chic.

Abanicos elegantes
Portaban con gentileza,
Y aretes ó dormilonas
Pasados por las orejas.

Sus caras muy repintadas
Con albayalde ó con cal,
Con ceniza ó velutina....
¡Pues vaya usté á adivinar!

Llevaban buenos corsés
Con pechos bien abultados
Y caderitas y muslos......
Postizos.... pues está claro.

El caso es que se miraban
Salerosas, retrecheras
Danzando al compas seguido
De música ratonera.

Se trataba, según dicen,
De efectuar alegre rifa
De un niño de catorce años,
Por colmo de picardías.

• Cuando más entusiasmados
Y quitados de la pena,
Se hallaban los mariquitos
Gozando de aquella fiesta

Púm! que los gendarmes entran
Sorprendiendo a los *jotones*!
Y aquello si fué de verse....
¡Qué apuros y que aflixiones!

Algunos quieren correr,
O echarse dentro el *común* ...
Otros quieren desnudarse
A otros les dá el patatús.

Una alarma general....
Lloran, chillan, y hasta ladran,
¡Qué rebumbio! ¡Qué conflictos!
Pero ninguno se escapa.

A todos, uno por uno
La policía los recoje,
Y á Tlapisquera derecho
Se los va llevando al trote.

cancioneros sang them and then had to run for their lives. One may take one's choice.

They are loosely classified, according to subject. Those that point morals or tell of saints and miracles, are known as *ejemplos*; those used for dancing are *sones*; while love songs, burlesques and satires are called *coplas*, or *versos*. *Relaciones* are more imaginative and are of fantastic happenings, put fables into the mouths of animals, or list in great detail the beauties of towns or regions. They laud popular heroes, describe picaresque adventures, or even rise to heights of allegory. The *tragedias*, as their name implies, describe public catastrophes or individual misfortunes. They are sung in a minor key with slow, dirge-like solemnity, in contrast to the usual *corrido* that has a gay, animated melody.

Each region has its own peculiar flavor; in the Huasteca district, for instance, *gritos de vaquero* (cowboy yells) and a peculiarly interesting falsetto are used in their *huapangos*, as they call their songs; in Vera Cruz, where they are noted for being sarcastic and biting, they are called *jarochos*, a name that derives from *jaro*, the long spear the Indios used to defend themselves against the Conquistadores.

Hipolito y Rosita, an identical twin of the North American folk-song *Frankie and Johnny*, gives a fair idea of the native crudity of many *corridos*.

HIPOLITO Y ROSITA

Polito crashed the fandango,
Pushed folks from his way without care,
Outran his friends and relations
And everyone else who was there.

He put his hand in his pocket
A kerchief as if to pull out
Rosita regarded him sadly
Then sighed and slow turned about.

He dropped a quick hand to his belt.
And suddenly pulled out his gun.
There, as she sat without moving,
He gave her three shots; she was done.

11

Then in rushed Rosita's poor papa,
And asked in a sort of a groan
What has happened to you, Rosita,
I was sure that I heard you moan?

Trist clink of Guadalajara
Some seven strong walls has this jail
Where men for life are imprisoned
Because women are faithless—frail.[1]

Sometimes, however, charming bits of sensitive verse like *La Locomotora* are found.

The locomotive passes here,
Conductors with caps and watches bright
What pleases me more are the small carts
Of the valley where first I saw light.

[1] From 'El Romance Espanol y el Corrido Mexicano' por Vicente Mendoza; Ediciones de la Universidad Nacional de Mexico, Mexico City, 1939, p. 499.
The translation is by Edward Larocque Tinker.

'EL VALIENTE DE GUADALAJARA'

The 'half-horse half-alligator' tradition of the American river boatman and the boast of the American cowboy that he was woolly below the knees had their counterpart in Mexico in the artistic boasting of the *valiente* from Guadalajara. Like the Tall Texan, the Guadalajaran or *tapatío* was a widely known and often satirized type.

The Guadalajara bravo claims to be wild, though not woolly; he is not a horse or an alligator, but he does assert that he is a tiger, or at the very least a panther. The tiger facing the *tapatío* in Posada's print is not his adversary but the *tapatío* himself, as he appears in the picture he paints for the crowd. In actual life these boasts—often the prelude to bloody fights—had their ritualistic formality, depending heavily on proverbial phrases and other folk terminology which both the opponent and the admiring audience understood.

What the broadside poet has done here is to take a number of typical boasts and string them together, finding his rhymes where he could, often using proper names to provide the needed rhyme. The verse form is that of the *décima*, a ten-line stanza usually rhyming ABBAACCDDC, rather than the *corrido* quatrain, but the introduction is made up of two quatrains.

12

II : *Translation on page 43*

EL VALIENTE
DE GUADALAJARA.

Entrenle al Gualajareño
Antes que se le haga tarde;
Mire que no es un cobarde,
Y sí el mentado Briseño,

No soy como el potosino;
Ni jamás he sido arreado;
Soy del barrio de Santiago
Y no distingo padrino.

Si porque traigo pechera
Figuran que soy arriero,
Piensan que soy un ranchero
Porque porto calzonera;
Aunque vea yo á la pantera,
Nunca se me arruga el cuero
Por que no conozco el miedo;
Ya tu lo has visto, Tagarno,
Que á ninguno le recelo
Aunque fuere Zamorano.

No tengo el modo tan feo,
Y me atoro en cualquier gancho;
Y por doquier que paseo,
Donde quiera lavo y plancho.
No crean que bajé del rancho,
Ni que me peleo en cuadrilla,
Vengo buscando á la *ardilla*
Por que no sabe plagiar,
Aunque es la fiebre amarilla
La contra le vengo á dar.

Por Jalisco me paseé
Y hasta les eché la pela;
Solito yo la brillé
Por el barrio "La Canela,"
Ya tú lo has visto, Manuela,
Que yo nunca soy dejado;
A Jesús Castro he encontrado
Que estaba abrazando á Pancha:
Me vió y me dijo enojado:
Que no te calientas plancha?

Una vida es la que tengo,
La misma que he de dejar,
Si creen que me ando durmiendo
Todos se han de equivocar,
Jamás me sé yo aplomar,
Ni mucho menos me agüito
Aunque me vean chaparrito,
Mi alma nunca se cuartea,
Ya tu lo has visto. Irenea,
Que no le temo al prietito.

Al que no le guste el fuste
Que lo tire y monte en pelo;
Aquí está, Calzón de cuero,
Y nunca crean que se asuste
Pues aquel que no le guste
Que me hable por derechito.
¿Es verdad vale bonito
Que no traigo chiquihuite?
Por hay anda el changomite
Que les trae su bocadito.

Soy tapatío muy famoso,
He andado bien la Nación,
Buscando algún fanfarrón
De los que anden por aquí,
Por Colima y por Tepic
Busqué á los de mucho tino,
Hasta el mejor potosino
Le di pruebas de hombresote;
No busco hermano ni tío,
Aquí traigo mi garrote.

TIERNAS SUPLICAS

CON QUE INVOCAN LAS JOVENES DE 40 AÑOS

AL MILAGROSO SAN ANTONIO DE PADUA

PIDIENDOLE SU CONSUELO

San Antonio milagroso, | Que me des un buen esposo
Yo te suplico llorando, | Por que ya me estoy pasando.

San Antonio bendecido.
Santo de mi devoción.
Por tu santa intercesión
Dame, por Dios; un marido.
Sea viejo, manco ó tullido,
Que me quiera en todo caso,
Y si no un soldado raso
O un recluta de cuartel
Para casarme con él:
¡Qué me paso! ¡qué me paso!

No te pido un general,
Duque, conde ni marqués,
Que lo que yo quiero, es,
Un hombre que sea formal;
Sea el ladrón más criminal,
El caso es tener marido;
Ya ves cuanto he padecido
En el materno regazo:
¡Oh San Antonio querido!
¡No ves, no ves que me paso!

Santo misericordioso;
Te lo pido y en tì espero,
Que me dés un compañero,
¡Un esposo, un buen esposo!
Aunque sea viejo gotoso,
Nada me importa el frentazo,
Por que nadie me hace caso,
Me huyen como á Lucifer:
¡Piedad para esta mujer!...
¡Mira, Santo, qué me paso!

Por tu santa caridad,
¡Oh San Antonio bendito!
Ten de mi piedad, piedad,
Por tu poder infinito.
Dame siquiera un viudito
Que me dé un buen di untazo,
No me pongas largo plazo
Arregla mi matrimonio,
Cásame con el demonio
¡Porque si no yo me paso!

Thousands of flights of gay birds
Go flying by here and by there.
What pleases me more are the sad doves
Of the valley where first I knew care.[2]

The *cancioneros* traveled alone, or in pairs, and in the larger cities they teamed up in small bands of seven or eight, called *mariachis*, and chanted their songs to the accompaniment of *violines*, *jaranas*, *guitarras*, *guitrrones*, and sometimes small drums. They played at fiestas, markets, cockpits, cantinas, or anywhere crowds congregated, and were hired as ambassadors of Cupid by enamored swains to play in the moonlight under their *novias'* window. They dressed in the elaborately picturesque charro costume, and earned the name of *mariachis* in an amusing way. When Maximilian was Emperor of Mexico many of his French soldiers married native girls, and musicians played at the wedding feast. They officiated at so many of these *mariages*, as the French called them, that the bands became known as *mariachis*, which was as near as the peon tongue could come to pronouncing the French word.

The majority of the *corridos* were passed on by word of mouth, for they were the work of illiterate folk blessed with the knack of

[2] From 'El Romance Espanol y el Corrido Mexicano' por Vincente Mendoza; Ediciones de la Universidad Nacional de Mexico, Mexico City, 1939, p. 499.
  The translation is by Edward Larocque Tinker.

'TIERNAS SÚPLICAS'

Jokes about old maids are not as common in the United States as they were in the days before women's rights, when a woman's only purpose in life was to marry and raise a family. In Mexico the old customs have lived on; even today some girls feel that to remain single is a woman's greatest shame. Mexican folklore has been rich in comic songs about tender young virgins of forty or so who are getting desperate about their chances of catching a husband, and who year after year lower the minimum of their expectations. The saint to whom old maids pray for husbands is St. Anthony of Padua, the same who gave the city of San Antonio, Texas, its name. This broadside is in the *letrilla* form, the lines of each stanza culminating in a refrain, 'I'm overripe! I'm overripe!' Posada has added a grotesque collection of 'overripe' types in his illustration.

15

III : *Translation on page 45*

impromptu verse, inherited from their Spanish peasant forebears. But the more popular ones were printed on broadsheets, decorated with crude illustrations, and the cancioneros peddled them to their audiences for a few *centavos* a piece.

One family was famous in this business for three generations, and well earned the title of 'printer to the populace,' for they supplied the humble with what they wanted—printed plays and prayers, naive hagiographies, children's stories, cheap periodicals, and passionate love-notes for the unlettered, that needed only to be signed and sent. This little press was set up in Mexico City, in 1880, by Don Antonio Vanegas Arroyo, and is conducted today by his son, Blas, and his grandson, Arsacio. To make sure that he would have a sufficient supply of new *corridos* always on hand, Don Antonio subsidized a facile poet Constancio S. Suárez to write verses about passing events. Two artists illustrated them, one of

'VERSOS MUY EXTRAVAGANTES'

This broadside is in a very old European tradition which includes not only the animal ballad but the animal tale as well. In English one need only mention 'Froggie Went A'Courtin'' and 'Fiddle-De-Dee.' Spain gave to Mexico similar songs, such as 'El Casamiento del Piojo y la Pulga' (The Wedding of the Louse and the Flea), to which tradition was added the propensity in Indian myth and tale to see animals as half-human. It is no accident that Don Coyote, as J. Frank Dobie has called him, is the principal figure in this song. As 'El Corrido de los Animales,' the Vanegas Arroyo broadside is widespread in oral tradition. Down to the present day, in Mexico and the American Southwest, the antics of the animals have amused children and adults alike. Vanegas Arroyo hired popular poets who wrote many of the ballads he published, but other broadsides were based on pieces current in the oral tradition of the provinces. The 'Versos Muy Extravagantes' seems to belong in this second group.

From the point of view of form the broadside exemplifies the transition between an older form, the *décima*, and the true *corrido* with its four-line stanza. The melody to which 'El Corrido de los Animales' is usually sung is one of four musical members, in ternary time, a *corrido* tune which corresponds with the two introductory quatrains. To sing the ten-line *décimas* that follow, a ritornello is made on the last two lines to cover the first six lines of the *décima* and then the tune is repeated to cover the final four. The opening quatrains, it should be noted, are ABAB and in the *corrido* pattern instead of the ABBA of the quatrains introducing most *décimas*.

16

IV : *Translation on page 46*

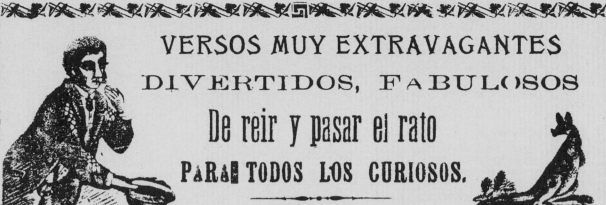

VERSOS MUY EXTRAVAGANTES
DIVERTIDOS, FABULOSOS
De reir y pasar el rato
PARA TODOS LOS CURIOSOS.

Iba llegando un coyote
A la gran ciudad de Leon,
Cuando llegó un Zopilote
Que andaba de Comisión.

Y le dijo en la calzada,
Oiga amigo zá donde va
Con esa mujer casada?
Ahora me la pagará.

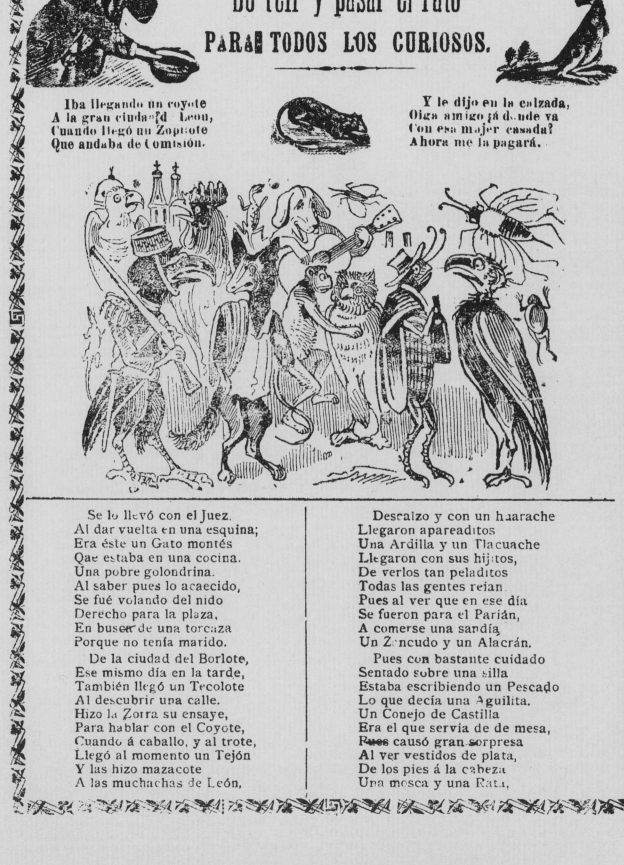

Se lo llevó con el Juez.
Al dar vuelta en una esquina;
Era éste un Gato montés
Que estaba en una cocina.
Una pobre golondrina.
Al saber pues lo acaecido,
Se fué volando del nido
Derecho para la plaza,
En busca de una torcaza
Porque no tenía marido.

De la ciudad del Borlote,
Ese mismo día en la tarde,
También llegó un Tecolote
Al descubrir una calle.
Hizo la Zorra su ensaye,
Para hablar con el Coyote,
Cuando á caballo, y al trote,
Llegó al momento un Tejón
Y las hizo mazacote
A las muchachas de León.

Descalzo y con un huarache
Llegaron apareaditos
Una Ardilla y un Tlacuache
Llegaron con sus hijitos,
De verlos tan peladitos
Todas las gentes reian.
Pues al ver que en ese día
Se fueron para el Parián,
A comerse una sandía,
Un Zancudo y un Alacrán.

Pues con bastante cuidado
Sentado sobre una silla
Estaba escribiendo un Pescado
Lo que decía una Aguilita.
Un Conejo de Castilla
Era el que servia de de mesa,
Pues causó gran sorpresa
Al ver vestidos de plata,
De los pies á la cabeza
Una mosca y una Rata,

En esto no cabe duda
Que todos tienen su maña.
Como dijo la tortuga
A la Hormiga y á la Araña:
Vámonos todos mañana
Con el amigo coyote,
Entonces dijo el jicote:
Yo también los acampaño
Porque me gusta el mitote,
Nomás me aguardan un año.

¡Qué tantos son doce meses
Dijo un coruco borracho,
Dejamos ya de sandeces,
Vamos echando otro cacho,
Cuando á poco llegó un macho
Montado en una cotorra
¿Pues qué sucede chamorra?
Le dijo una lagartija,
Luego que Dios me socorra
Me voy á casar con su hija.

Luego llegó un pinacate
Con su botella en la mano
De guante con un mallate
Con un sombrero jaraño,
Todos llegaron temprano
Siempre buscando al coyote
También llegó un guajolote,
Pero convertido en mole,
En las tranvías llegó al trote
Un cochino hecho posole.

Se juntó con la reunión
Hasta no verles el fin,
Así dijo un chapulín
De sorbete y bastón
Cuando les dió la canción
Un tordo y un armadillo
Se fueron al Baratillo,
A comprar unos anteojos,
Para espulgar al Zorrillo
Porque tenía muchos piojos.

Se caía muerto de risa
Un pícaro gavilán
De verse ya sin camisa,
Pero sí con buen gabán.
Un perico en un zahuán
Estaba echando tortillas,
Las calandias amarillas
Pusieron el nixtamal
Pues como ya no hay cuartillas
Les hecharon harta cal

Les dijo una culebrona
Pues allá todito vale,
Vámonos para Cantoya
Para que á todos les cale,
Nos llevamos á mi vale
Al gallo y también la polla,
Seguro que ahora se empolla
Porque no trae polizón
Vaya y dele parte á Moya
Por tan bonita reunión.

Como decentes personas
Todos llegaron en coche
Un zenzontle una paloma,
Un gorrión y un huitlacoche,
Ese mismo día en la noche
Hicieron un gran fandango
Una lechuza y un chango
Bailaron puritos schotis,
Cuando les dijo el coyote
¡Ah qué gesto se andan dando!

En fin la liebre ligera
También llegó de partida
Con una cierva cuerera,
Y una perrita parida;
Como era tan concurrida
Todita la reunión,
Se fueron á una función
Ya todita la pacota,
Y bailando la mascota
Pasaron todos por León.

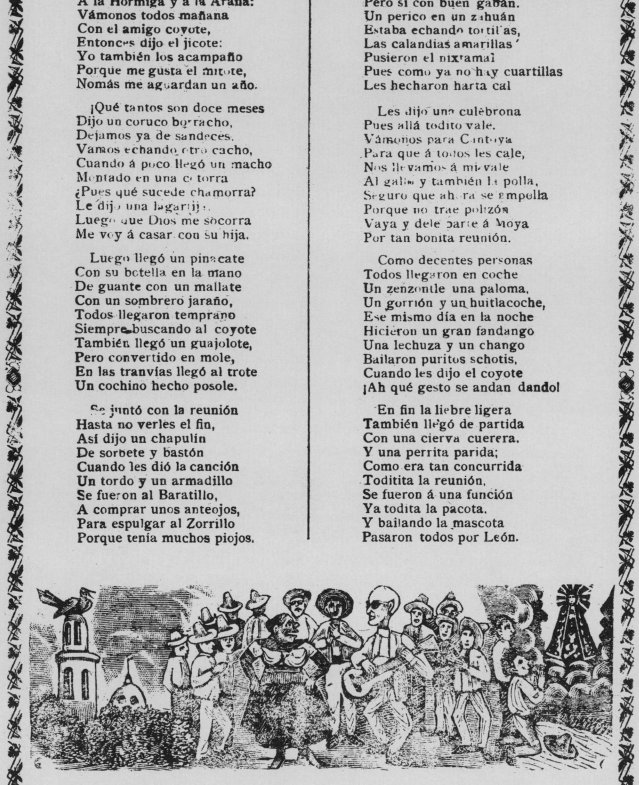

12
R.—Siglo XX Año 1903 México—Imprenta de A Vanegas Arroyo, 5ª de Lecumberri 2597

whom, JOSE GUADALUPE POSADA, was destined to become famous. He was born in Aguascalientes in 1851, and as a young man, moved to León where he taught school and was employed in an engraver's shop between times. When the flood of 1887 wrecked the city, he moved to the capital where he went to work for the Vanegas Arroyos.

His industry was superhuman, and he permitted himself but one relaxation. Every day he put aside fifty centavos until he had saved enough to buy two kegs of the excellent León tequila, for which the town is famous. He never broached them until Christmas day when he began his celebration of the New Year. During January he continued his libations and consumed the last drop on the last day of the month. For the balance of the year he neither drank nor smoked.

Both Posada and his employers were fearless, crusading spirits, always ready to fight for reforms, or poke fun at dishonest officials in decorticating verses adorned with caricatures. As a consequence they were often thrown into jail—not a pleasant experience in those days when conditions in Belén prison were notorious. One lampooned politician was too incensed to leave vengeance to the authorities, so he went to the printing shop late one night and, with the help of twenty henchmen, wrecked the presses and scattered the type in the street.

Posada had an inexhaustible fund of ideas and his work, while crude, had tremendous vitality and power. No one knew better how to catch the public eye. Like Daumier, his ruthless pen sketched the common denominator of an entire class in a few decisive lines.

Diego Rivera used to go to his studio as a small boy, and called him 'the interpreter of the sorrows, the happiness, and the agonized aspirations of the Mexican people', and added that he was 'a tenacious, mocking, and ferocious combatant'.

Posada was particularly famous for the macabre imagination and horripilating humor of his illustrations for *calaveras*—a word that has the double meaning of 'skull' and 'scatterbrain'. It is also the name given to the traditional poems composed for 'All Souls' Day', an important holiday in most Catholic countries.

This fiesta dates back to the 11th century when the Church set the day aside for prayers for those who had died in the faith. In Mexico, the celebration begins with the presentation in theatres all over the country, of José Zorrilla's *Don Juan Tenorio* that is in

19

harmony with the occasion because of its grim humor, and the spectres that materialize on the stage.

On 'El Día de los Chiquitos Difuntos' (The Day of the Dead Children) the cemeteries are crowded with Indios and superstitious people who spread toys, lighted candles, and food on their family tombs. They eat *mole* and drink *pulque*, in a belief they share with peasants in some parts of Europe, that the souls of their departed return to take a vicarious interest in the feast. Everything is on a cheerful note and there is no morbidity, for the Mexican mind accepts death with philosophy, and even nonchalance—a philosophy perhaps rooted in pre-Columbian Indio influence. Aztec thought regarded the ending of life, not as a catastrophe, but rather as a completion or fulfillment, Aztec art employed macabre motifs, Aztec rites included human sacrifice, and two Aztec festivals for the dead are described in Padre Sahagún's famous *History of Ancient Mexico*; so it may well be that the deep significance that in Mexico attaches to All Saints' week is because the Christian rite

'CALAVERAS'

There is a statue of Coatlicue, Aztec mother of the gods, which has survived from pre-Columbian times. Her face is a skull, with two rows of big, even teeth. Her robe is adorned with skulls, and on her head is a crown of skulls. Posada could have designed her for one of his *Calavera* broadsides. Spanish folk customs connected with All Souls' Day combined with Aztec practices to produce the *Calaveras*. Two other European elements have played a part: the art works of medieval and Renaissance Europe depicting Judgment Day or developing the *memento mori* theme and the *pasquín*.

It is said that Cortés, during a lull between battles with the Indians, discovered some scurrilous verses written on a wall, criticizing his conduct of the campaign. Cortés composed some verses of his own, in answer, and had them written upon the same wall. During the colonial period the pasting of these *pasquines* on the walls of public buildings was an accepted practice. They spared no one, not even the viceroys. At least one viceroy saw fit to order a reply. During the 19th century the *Calaveras* took over the functions of the *pasquín*, except that in the *Calaveras* the lampoon is always cast into the form of a mock epitaph. Their two main functions are to remind us in a good-humored way that we all are mortal, and to poke fun at friends and attack public officials. These last are supposed to take it all in good grace. *Calaveras* are still published every November 1 in many cities of Mexico, and in some cities in Texas, notably San Antonio.

20

v : *Translation on page 49*

CALAVERAS EN MONTON

AL PRECIO DE UN DECIMAL

Como nunca se habrá visto

EN TODA ESTA CAPITAL

 Es una verdad sincera
Lo que nos dice esta frase:
Que sólo el ser que no nace
No puede ser calavera.

Esto es una ensaladilla
Para todos los mortales,
Porque hasta los militares
Les ha de dar pesadilla.

 Es calavera el inglés,
Calavera, sí señor,
Calavera fué el frances
Y Faure y Sadi Carnot.
El Chino, el Americano,
El Papa y los Cardenales,
Reyes, duques, consejales
Y el jefe de la nación
En la tumba son iguales
Calaveras del montón.

Calavera el general
Y todos sus ayudantes,
Coroneles, comandantes
Y el furioso capitán.
Los subalternos serán
Calaveras en dos tiempos;
En uno son los sargentos,
Los cabos en pelotón,
Los soldados son por cientos
Calaveras del montón.

Toditos los comerciantes
Vendrán á ser calaveras
Porque ahora sí es deveras
Se acabó la Jauja de ántes,
Los cómicos resabidos
Que en todo son presumidos,
Huesos roidos y podridos
Los dueños de tendajón
Y todo dueño de giros,
Calaveras del montón.

Calavera el maromero
De cualquier circo en función,
Dueños de fonda ó mesón,
De botica ó de allí enfrente,
Todo el que engaña á la gente
Que vende todo barato;
El baratillero ingrato
Por egoista y por ahorcón
El empeñero y el beato,
Calaveras del montón.

A todos los que yo veo
Vendiendo velas de cera,
Son horribles calaveras
Que ruedan por el recreo,
Mómias secas del museo
Son toditos los neveros,
Los dulceros, pasteleros
Y fruteros en unión,
Sean también los mamoneros
Calaveras del montón.

Toditas las chimoleras
Son calaveras en mole
Y las que hacen chacualole
Juntas con las tamaleras,
Que sigan las tortilleras
Por chorreadas y liendrudas,
Las carniceras sin duda
Por vender mal chicharrón
Y el que comercia en verdura
Calaveras del montón.

MÉXICO.—IMPRENTA DE ANTONIO VANEGAS ARROYO, CALLE DE SANTA TERESA NÚM. 1.

Los mártires borrachitos
Rateros tan chiquititos
Y el pobre de Arnulfo Arroyo
Que me lo echaron al hoyo,
Todos los papeleritos
Tirándose en duro suelo,
¡Cuánta aflición sin consuelo
Si están crudos ó en prisión,
Justo es que vayan al cielo
Sin ser huesos del moutón.

Calaveras las mujeres,
Mujeres no más de nombre
Que les gusta tener hombre
Y no cumplir sus deberes,
Amantes de los placeres,
Que son pocas las honradas
Las más son flacas, son locas,
Y pediches por pilón
Aunque sean de hábito y toca
Calaveras del montón.

Calaveras infernales
Son las maldecidas viudas
Traidoras aún peor que Júdas
Hipócritas y desleales.
Aparentan sufrir males
Cuando el muerto está tendido
Pero si han visto al querido
Les dá mal de corazón
Y dicén: es mi marido
Calavera del montón.

Los ricos por su elegancia
Los rotitos con redrojos,
Los pobres por su miseria,
Los tontos por su ignorancia
Los jóvenes por su infancia
Los hombres de edad madura
Todos en la sepultura
Con las viejas ¡¡qué aflicción!!
Serán como dice el cura:
Calaveras del montón.

Ya se me había olvidado
Enumerar mis parientes,
Siendo héroes tan excelentes
Cual mi tío el jorobado.
Mi primo el cojo me ha dado
Mi golletito y mi muerto,
Mi sobrino, manco y tuerto,
Llora sin consolación,
Porque es por su desacierto
Calavera del montón.

Calaveras elegantes
Son todos los magistrados
Los médicos ó abogados
Y también los estudiantes,
También son los practicantes
Del hospital y enfermeros,
Y los jueces más severos
Que fallan sin compasión,
Que sean con los carceleros
Calaveras del montó.

En fin, el compositor
Que versos no supo hacer,
No habrá quien llore por él
Pues antes dirán mejor:
Ya se murió el bablador
Que nos ponía mil defectos,
Que se lo coman los puercos
Pues no merece panteón
Y que sea entre tantos muertos
Calavera del montón.

La cocinera chorreada,
La loca recamarera,
La faceta costurera,
La pilmama por arreada;
Y la niña Sofía Ahumada
Que se echó de Catedral.
Y todas en general
Por su mala inclinación,
Serán por su fin fatal,
Calaveras del montón.

Las pelonas y alisadas
Con manteca relumbrosas
Tan cuscas y revoltosas,
Y las que andan replanchadas
Indiotas, patas rajadas,
Peinadas con agua-cola,
Toditas las de la bola
Con las viejas del rincón,
Aquí sí hago carambola
Calaveras del montón.

Las horribles cacarizas,
Las chatas y las getonas,
Las altas por tan zanconas,
Las chaparras por erizas,
Las prietas por tan cenizas,
Las blancas por melindrosas
Las flacas por pegajosas
Y las gordas por visión,
Que sean todas horrorosas
Calaveras del montón.

GRAN
BAILE
DE
CALAVERAS.

Llegó la gran ocasión
De divertirse deveras,
Van á hacer las calaveras
Su fiesta en el Panteón.

Las tumbas se han adornado,
Los sepulcros se han barrido,
Los féretros se han pulido
Y las lozas barnizado;

Los festejos sepulcrales,
Muchas horas durarán;
Los muertos asistirán
Con vestidos especiales.

Con gran anticipación
Calaveras y esqueletos
Se han hecho trajes completos
Que luzcan en la reunión.

México Imprenta de Antonio Vanegas Arroyo Calle de Santa Teresa núm 1 —1906.

En las glorietas mejores
Habrá kermess con sus puestos;
Y locales bien dispuestos;
Donde estén los bailadores

En el centro se ha arreglado
Un salón para la danza,
La primera contradanza
Previamente se ha ensayado.

Y en ella tomarán parte
Los más encumbrados muertos,
La mesa, de mil cubiertos,
Será servida con arte.

En ella se ofrecerán
Manjares extraordinarios,
Gusanos en guisos varios,
Con petróleo y alquitrán.

Muchos vinos espumosos,
"Lágrimas evaporadas"
De viuditas consoladas
Y de herederos forzosos.

Los blandones funerarios
Iluminarán la fiesta;
Habrá numerosa orquesta
Escogida en las osarios.

Las flautas son de canillas,
De hueso son los violines,
De cráneos los cornetines,
Los fagots de rabadillas

También se pondrá Ambigú
Con focos de luz chinescos,
Allí se darán refrescos
A toda la multitud.

Para los muertos menudos,
Los de tecones de hueso,
Habrá pulque, hasta el exceso,
Y hojitas, para los crudos.

Mucho antes de la función
Todos los muertos pudientes,
Se han hecho trajes lucientés
Y dignos de la ocasión.

Las indias, huepil bordado
Con hilos de mil colores;
Los charros, los aguadores,
Sombreros muy galoneados.

Un licenciado famoso
Que tres fortunas robó
Estrenará frac punzó
Y un calzado primoroso.

Un militar esforzado
Que en todas partes corría,
La gran cruz de valentía
Lucirá muy estirado.

Las viuditas relamidas
Que se precian de virtuosas,
Asistirán, ruborosas,
Todas de blanco vestidas.

Los sastres no dan abasto
Para tanta petición.
Cada cual en la función
Quiero solo hacer el gasto.

—¿A donde vas calavera
Que te sales del osario?
—Apártese el temerario,
Que no soy una cualquiera.

Voy á ver á mi modista
Que mi sudario me cosa;
Me voy á poner hermosa,
Con mi blusa nunca vista.

—Adiós linda calavera
De mirar tan retrechero
¿Me quieres mucho?
—¡Te quiéro!
¡Hasta que de nuevo muera!

Esta noche en la balumba
Seremos uno los dos....
—¡Hasta la noche!....
—¡Sí adios!
Te espero junto á mi tumba

—Tras de tu cariño voy
Y si lograrlo no acierto,
Verás que me caigo muerta....
Más muerto de lo que estoy.

—No te hagas falta de oído
Calavera salerosa......
—Déjeme..... que en esa fosa,
Está viendo mi marido.

—Oye muerta zandunguera
Que luces esa mortaja
Donde brilla tanta alhaja,
¿Quieres ser mi compañera?

Así, en confuso vaivén,
Se chancean los esqueletos,
Mientras aguardan inquietos
Que principie el somatén.

Los sudarios se reforman,
Se remiendan las mortajas
Y con las fúnebres cajas
Estrado y gradas se forman.

Allí irán los abogados
Con toda su vanidad;
Allí irá la Facultad
Y los Doctores borlados.

En revuelta confusión
Estarán las calaveras,
Y las meras petateras
Disfrutarán la ocasión.

Será una gran igualdad
Que nivele grande y chico;
No habrá ni pobre rico
En aquella sociedad.

De este mundo en la extensión
El oro á todos pervierte,
Pero despues de la muerte
No hay clases ni condición.

Y bailarán chimoleras
Con los pollos bien vestidos;
Todos estarán unidos,
Todos serán calaveras.

Bailarán los comerciantes,
Los sastres y los cocheros,
Los soldados, los pulqueros,
Albañiles y estudiantes.

Ingenieros y cantores,
Dependientes y modistas,
Carretoneros, y artistas,
Lavanderas y pintores.

Hasta el pobre borrachín,
El de la pata rajada,
Se dará la gran armada
Bebiendo champaña y Rin.

Irán desde las señoras,
Hasta las gatas ladinas
Las más rudas, las más finas,
Gozarán por muchas horas.

Será de ver el meneo
Que se arme al anochecer;
Cada muerto á su placer,
Cada muerta de jaleo.

—¡No la raspe, licenciado....!
—¡Echele vino á la chata....!
—¡No venga á meter la pata....!
—¡Otra de pulque curado....!

—Aquí no es como el mundo,
Sitio de llanto y pasiones....
Aquí hay leales corazones....!
Aquí el cariño es profundo!

Y así entre bromas y cantos,
Y danzones y conciertos,
Se pasan muy bien los muertos
La noche de Todos Santos.

El que quiera, la función
Mirar de las calaveras....
Que se muera de deveras
Y se vaya al Panteón.

took root in a pagan Indio psychology peculiarly attuned by inheritance to accept it.

This may also explain why sugar symbols of death in endless variety are sold in the *dulcerías* and market-places at this time: sticks of candy shaped like leg-bones, pallid skeletons reposing in chocolate coffins, and sugar skulls that clack their jaws horrendously when a thread is pulled. There are even elaborate candy models of funeral-trains, with realistic plumes and black draperies, filled with mourners; or miniature cemetery plots complete with tomb, corpse, a weeping willow and even a weeping widow clad in licorice mourning. These grisly gifts are exchanged in the same spirit as our valentines.

On the last day of the celebration the flower shops and market stalls overflow with gigantic wreaths and crosses, many of them made with the *Flor de muerto* that resembles the North American marigold. The churches are crowded early, and after prayers have been said for the dead, the rest of the day is devoted to fun and fiesta, *bailes* and bullfights, meals and *mariachis*.

Only at this time of the year do the *calaveras* appear to add their sardonic flavor to the gaiety of the occasion. Printed on colored paper, adorned with the grisly insignia of death, they carry verses satirizing people in the public eye, speaking of them as though they were dead, and often ending with burlesque epitaphs. They are peddled on the streets and read in cafés with many a chuckle. The newspapers, too, take this opportunity to run caricatures and caustic verses in *calavera* vein, about politicians and government officials against whom they have some grudge.

No one illustrated these better than Posada, for his grotesque improvisations, fertility of imagination, and the human quality he imparted to his grinning, dancing cadavers, made him the supreme master of this kind of work. Another talent he possessed was for depicting the life and types of his countrymen—a genius he used to arouse the public conscience to realization of the wrongs of the down-trodden. These qualities combined to make him the greatest single inspiration in the artistic development of Diego Rivera and José Clemente Orozco. He focused the attention of the entire modern school, that grew up around them, on their own Indio-Spanish culture, and showed where to seek for inspiration.

After a life of unbelievable productivity, in the course of which

25

he made some fifteen thousand plates, Posada died, in 1913, an impecunious and relatively obscure artist; but his stature has grown with the years and an exhibition of one thousand prints, held in the Palacio de Bellas Artes, in Mexico City, sealed his fame for all time.

For more than two centuries, troubadors strolled through Mexico, singing the news and tales of high romance in *pueblecitos* isolated from every other form of amusement; and their songs became the voice of the peon soul, a true Indo-Spanish folk-culture.

During the Revolution, the hopes and aspirations of the illiterate poor found expression in innumerable *corridos* that celebrated victorious generals and battles won; and these, taken together, presented a crude, racy, and impressive history of the rebellion, that had an impact and popular appeal only a folk-art, rooted in the soil, could give.

'EL MOSQUITO AMERICANO'

Another *letrilla*, using the title as a refrain. 'The American mosquito'—that is, the mosquito of the New World in distinction to that of other parts of the globe—had been much in the news in the years prior to 1904, when this broadside appeared. Around the turn of the century the 'mosquito americano' had been the object of a determined campaign on the part of the U.S. Medical Corps in Cuba. In 1904 another battle was beginning against the mosquito in connection with the building of the Panama Canal. North American preoccupation with the insect provided an interesting topic of conversation for the Mexican folk, as ded the amusing American belief that the mosquito had something to do with *paludismo* (malaria). These topical references undoubtedly were in the broadside poet's mind. But the bothersome pest he writes about is a 'Yankee' mosquito, which has entered from the United States through Laredo, Texas, and spread the length and breadth of Mexico. It is difficult to ascertain what American 'invasion' of Mexico the broadside refers to; the American tourist was a comparatively rare animal in the Mexico of 1904. Many Mexicans, however, were opposed to the Díaz policy of bringing in American technicians to develop the Mexican economy. The common folk too were often hostile toward American innovations. During the remodeling of the Mexico City Cathedral in 1905, when the old clock mentioned in the next broadside was taken down, a rumor swept Mexico that the Cathedral was being sold to American speculators, who would convert it either into a Protestant church or a factory. Posada shows us the 'American mosquito' attacking all classes, the straw-hatted peon and the silk-hatted gentleman alike. 'Mosca' (fly) is a Mexican slang term for 'money.' The 'American mosquito' may have been the American dollar.

26

VI : *Translation on page 50*

EL MOSQUITO AMERICANO

El mosquito americano
Ahora acaba de llegar;
Dicen se vino á pasear
A este suelo mexicano.

Dizque el Domingo embarcó
Allá en Laredo de Texas,
Y que al Saltillo llegó
Picándoles las orejas.
En la estación á unas viejas
Qué bien las hizo marchar,
Hasta las hizo sudar
Este animal inhumano;
Luego empiezan á gritar:
El Mosquito americano.

A Guanajuato marchó:
Esto es cosa de reír;
El al centro no llegó,
Pero sí estuvo en Marfil:
Ya no lo podían sufrir
Tan malcriado y altanero,
Pues le picó en el trasero
A un militar veterano,
Porque es mucho, muy grosero
El Mosquito americano.

Tomó el rumbo de Irapuato
Y por Pénjamo pasó;
De allí luego regresó
Por el pueblo de Uriangato.
La hacienda de Villachato
La dejó muy derrotada;
Toda la gente asustada
La encontró el vale Mariano,
Nana Emeteria gritaba:
El Mosquito americano,

Por la puerta de San Juan,
Piedra Gorda y la Sandía,
Una viejita decía:
¡Jesús, qué fiero animal!
Dígame usted, Don Pascual
¿No le ha llegado el mosquito?
Dicen que es muy chiquitito,
Y también muy inhumano;
¿Qué dice tata Pachito
El mosquito americano?

Versos de Valentín Mancera

TRAIDOS DEL ESTADO DE GUANAJUATO

AÑO DE MIL OCHOCIENTOS OCHENTA Y DOS MUY PRESENTE

MURIO

VALENTIN MANCERA

MURIO EL ESPADA VALIENTE

¡Ay! qué dolor
lleva en su corazón
de ver que nadie
le tiene compasión.
Se repite al fin de cada cuarteta

El diez y nueve de Marzo
a las cuatro de la mañana,
se ha dirigido al oficio
la desgraciada San Juana.

Muy buenos días mi señor
don Dionisio Catalán
ahí le tengo su prenda
la que busca de San Juan.

Lo sacaron entre cuatro
con mucho gusto y afán
lo llevaron que lo viera,
don Dionisio Catalán.

Le empezaron a tocar
al compás de la guitarra,
las agonías de la muerte
porque lo vendió San Juana.

A este Valentín Mancera
¡ah qué suerte le tocó!
lo mataron a balazos....
el gobierno lo mandó.

Respondió la pobre madre:
señores, ¿que harán favor?
que este Valentín Mancera
no muera sin confesión.

Los gachupines decían:
a nadie le hagan favor,
que a ese Valentín Mancera
ya le tenemos horror.

Este Valentín Mancera
¡ah qué suerte le ha tocado!
lo mataron a balazos
sin haberse confesado.

Este Valentín Mancera
era un hombre chaparrito,
no era alto, no era grueso....
era un poco delgadito.

De México lo pedía
todo el Ayuntamiento,
y el Presidente decía:
«a Valentín yo lo siento.»

Todos los gachupines
se vistieron de galón,
y estaban tomando copas
en la tienda del «Vapor.»

This was not a new manifestation, for, after every historical crisis —as when Mexico obtained her independence and when Juárez overthrew Maximilian—*corridos* had lighted the fires of nationalism; but this time their effect was more far-reaching than it had ever been before.

As a result of the *corridos* and of Posada's influence, the sophisticated artists and authors of Mexico, who had been slavish imitators of French and Spanish literary and artistic trends, were brought to realize, after the Revolution of 1910 was over, that these songs of the people, born of the freeing of long-pent emotions, reflected a re-awakened and passionate love of country and a new pride and confidence in their own civilization; and this persuaded them that here in their own backyard, in the sufferings of the lowly, lay subjects for their brush and pen; and that the leaders of their own revolution, made a far more forceful appeal to the imaginations of their countrymen than any heroes from Ulysses to Napoleon.

'VALENTÍN MANCERA'

The dates on this broadside are witness to one of the most important functions of presses like that of Vanegas Arroyo: their role in the revitalization of old ballads and the wider dissemination of ballads that had been restricted to one region alone. The title tells us that these are 'verses brought from the State of Guanajuato.' The first quatrain, printed as a subtitle under the scene depicting Mancera's execution, says that he died in 1882. The colophon tells us that Vanegas Arroyo printed the broadside in 1914.

In 1882 Porfirio Díaz was still engaged in pacifying the country, after having assumed power in the late 1870's. The process involved the capture and execution of many guerrilla leaders who had begun operations against the French during Maximilian's empire and had continued afterwards, some as out-and-out bandits, some as revolutionists attempting to overthrow the Díaz government who maintained themselves by looting and highway robbery. The first heroic *corridos* of Greater Mexico were composed about these outlaws.

In 1914 the Madero Revolution was almost four years old, and Mexico had been through its first year of bloody civil war. The heroic *corrido* was reaching its peak; Revolutionary *corridos* were being composed and sung in the manner witnessed by Edward Larocque Tinker when he was with Villa's troops before Celaya. 'Valentín Mancera' was one of the precursors of the Revolutionary *corrido,* just as its hero was a prototype of the Revolutionary guerrilla. The publication of this regional *corrido* by a Mexico City broadside press at the height of the Revolution must have been a factor in lengthening the life span and distribution of the ballad. It is still heard today among some Mexican folk groups in the United States.

29

VII : *Translation on page 51*

The artists were the first to react to this new and virile inspiration. José Clemente Orozco began painting the peon, giving plastic form to his hopes and sorrows and even to his social problems; while Diego Rivera, who lionized the proletariat, painted in the Ministry of Education a mural founded on *El Corrdo de la Revolución*, and still another on *El Corrido de Emilio Zapata*, that illustrate and translate into another medium the spirit and meaning of these folk songs. It was these two artists who gave impetus to a new autochthonous school that had repercussions in many parts of the Americas.

Their work is completely integrated in their own Indian culture, and their murals, colossal in scale, show the monolithic influence of Aztec stone sculpture. They deal with the impassive, patient, inscrutable Indio, and their explosive force, cruelty and bloody tragedy, suggest the more macabre work of Goya—qualities to be found in many of the murals commissioned by the Mexican Government for their public buildings.

Rivera's huge mural that decorates the wall behind the grandiose double stairway of the National Palace is a case in point. It was supposed to depict the history of Mexico, and I remember that when the President's protocol officer was showing me around, he pointed to the right of the mural, where a Conquistador in armor was roughly throwing an Indian maiden to the ground, and slyly said: 'There you see the beginnings of my race'.

Then came various scenes in Mexican history and portraits of

'DE LINO ZAMORA'

A *corrido* of the love-tragedy type taken by Vanegas Arroyo from the oral tradition of the provinces, as the subtitle indicates. Mendoza publishes a variant very close to this one in *El Romance Español y el Corrido Mexicano*, collected in Michoacán in 1936. In the first stanza Mendoza's variant reads, 'A *torero* killed him' rather than 'A bull killed him' as does the broadside. This last may be a misprint, since in both variants Lino Zamora is killed by his first *banderillero*. Or the broadside may have decided to play on words; the killer had been cuckolded by Zamora and could be thought of as wearing horns.

Corridos with refrains are relatively rare. The refrain in this one also narrates; its variations from stanza to stanza bring in narrative material that is essential to the progress of the story.

30

VIII : *Translation on page 53*

LEGITIMOS VERSOS

DE LINO ZAMORA,
TRAIDOS DEL REAL DE ZACATECAS

Pobre de Lino Zamora
¡Ah qué suerte le ha tocado!
Que en el Real de Zacatecas,
Un toro me lo ha matado.

Rosa, Rosita, Rosa Romero,
Ya murió Lino Zamora,
¡Qué haremos de otro torero!

Al salir de Guanajuato
Cuatro suspiros tiró,
En aquel cerro trozado
Su corazón le avisó,

Rosa, Rosita, Rosa Peruana,
Ya murió Lino Zamora;
La causa fué Prisciliana.

Y Lino le dijo á Braulio
Que se fuera hasta Jerez,
Que fuera á hacer la contrata
Y que volviera otra vez.

Rosa, Rosita, Rosa alelía,
Ya murió Lino Zamora,
Pues asi le convendría!

Cuando vino de Jerez
El jueves por la mañana,
Le dijo Martín su hermano:
Lino está con Prisciliana.

Rosita, Rosa Peruana,
Ya murió Lino Zamora
Por una mala tanteada.

El día catorce de Agosto,
Que era jueves por la tarde,
Se quedó Lino Zamora
Que era el primer espada.

En la calle de Tacuba
Estaba Lino parado,
Aquí te vas á morir,
Y aquí te quedas tirado.

Rosa Rosita, flor de clavel,
Ya murió Lino Zamora,
No lo volverás á ver!

Ese gracioso de Carmen
Pronto lo agarró del brazo,
Llegó el cobarde de Braulio
Y al pronto le dió el balazo

TRISTE Y DIVERTIDO DESPEDIMENTO
DEL RELOJ DE CATEDRAL
→ DE MEXICO. ←

El reloj de Catedral
Acabó su larga vida,
Y hoy le dá la despedida
A la hermosa capital.

El pobre viejo se vá
Llevándose de la historia
Páginas de duelo y gloria
Que jamás olvidará.

¡Adios México! El progreso
De tu bella capital,
Me relega por un mal
A un obligado receso.
Ya soy anciano y por eso
Me desechas de tu lado
Y me veré sentenciado
A que el hollín me destruya,
Y léjos de toda bulla
Pereceré arrinconado.

De la heróica Independencia
Presencié la lucha breve,
Y lo mismo cuando aleve
La ambición de una potencia,
Pretendió con insolencia
Levantar aquí su gallo,
Que quedó el cinco de Mayo
Cacareando y desplumado,
Pues aquí nunca ha floreado
La semilla del vasallo.

—

!Adios, el asta bandera,
Que sobre mí se apoyó,
Y en el que tanto flameó
Siempre hermosa y altanera.
Y entre todas la primera,
La enseña del pátrio suelo
Entre cuyo hermoso vuelo,
Ha recogido la historia
Páginas de inmensa gloria,
Lágrimas de amargo duelo.

¡Adios, queridas campanas
De las torres mis vecinas,
Cuyas notas cristalinas
Saludaba en las mañanas,
¡Adios, queridas hermanas!
Porque soy vieja me alejan,
Y que me lamente dejan
En ignorado destierro;
¡Tocad, tocad á mi entierro
Donde los muertos se añejan!

some of the heroes like Juárez and Porfirio Díaz. Next was a tremendous head of Karl Marx that fairly dominated the whole wall, and at the bottom of the picture, at the far left, was something that looked like a contribution box into which a long queue of ragged peones were dropping their *centavos*. A transparent pipe ran upwards from the box, through which the coins appeared to ascend and flow into the outstretched palm of a grossly revolting priest whose other arm was around the waist of an unmistakable wanton with one lush brown breast completely naked.

More money continued up through the pipe and cascaded in a huge pile on a table around which sat three men. One was the oil financier, Lord Cowdray, and one of the other two was John D. Rockefeller, Jr., who never knew he had been thus pilloried until I happened to tell him.

There were many other even more brutal and bloody Rivera murals in the buildings of the National University, and these had been defaced with nails as high as the more conservative students could reach; and, when I went to Guadalajara I was forced to lecture on Emerson and brotherly love standing in front of a Gargantuan mural by José Clemente Orozco, whose central figure was a huge diabolical *revolucionario* holding up a knife, dripping with blood, he had just plunged into a rather prosperous person who lay at his feet.

These qualities have appeared in the murals of many other public buildings. Done in a time of vindictive passions born of the Revolution, they are fierce, implacable political documents; but their implications work against Mexico's best interests, for they fan class hatreds, teach Marxian theories, attack religion, and breed excessive nationalism, just when the country needs the collaboration of all its people, and a sane attitude towards the United States.

'DEL RELOJ DE CATEDRAL'
A parody on the Spanish-language equivalent of the 'last goodnight.' Like the condemned criminal the clock recounts events in his past and says goodby to his friends, in this case the neighboring buildings. The broadside also is a satirical comment on contemporary events, the passing of an old Mexico City landmark. On the same vein is the composition added at the bottom of the sheet: a greeting to the new fifty-cent pieces issuel by the Díaz administration. Both are in the *décima* form.

33

IX : *Translation on page 55*

Nevertheless, these murals have importance as documents in the history of Mexican art, for Rivera and Orozco and their imitators played a vital part in liberating the art of their country from the bonds of classical European tradition. Yet their very fame has a tendency to enslave many of the younger men who follow them, to become little, and less talented, Orozcos and Riveras.

What is sorely needed now is a new brand of liberator to free Mexican art from the Aztec yoke and restore the balance between traditional European art, which is theirs through their Spanish ancestors, and the Indian heritage they today alone acknowledge.

*The recrudescence of the *corrido* revivified other arts and reinvigorated the language, proving the vitality and appeal of the life and sorrows of the populace as material for literature. A popular theatre, coarse, sordid, was spawned from these roots and trooped the country under tents but, when the intellectuals tried to found a *teatro revolucionario*, their dramas were mere ephemeral reviews, and failed dismally. Poets, even the most sophisticated, began expressing themselves in *corrido* form, and one of the best of the contemporaries, the Mexican ex-Ambassador, His Excellency Dr. Francisco Castillo Najera, wrote an epic *corrido grande—El gávilan*—the life story of an old revolutionist; while another well-known writer, Dr. Miguel N. Lira, a lawyer and college professor, is one of a long list of those who have conscientiously followed the folk ballad in metre and matter.

The music of the best composers has marked traces of corrido color, quality, and inspiration. Carlos Chávez' *Sinfonía proletaria* is based on their melodies, and the late Silvestre Revueltas drew

* Taken from *The Horsemen of the Americas and the Literature They Inspired*, by Edward Larocque Tinker, New York, Hastings House, 1953. (pp. 88 through 91)

'LOS LAMENTOS DE UN BORRACHITO'

Blue laws are not entirely an invention of the American Puritan mind, as we can see from this *corrido*, in which a dedicated drunkard laments the closing of Mexico City saloons and pulque shops on Sundays. The basic situation is universally known: the *borrachito* laments the fact that now he'll have to drink that awful stuff—water.

34

x : *Translation on page 56*

Los Lamentos de un Borrachito

Con motivo del cierre de Pulquerías y Cantinas.

¡Pos hora sí me amolé!
Nos va á llevar la *disgracia*;
Los domingos á las doce
Ya se acabó la parranda,

Se cierran las pulquerías
Y las cantinas también,
Y á retragar purita agua,
Purita agua como *guey*.

Yo que los domingos iba
Con mi *guitarra* á pasear,
Encachándonos medidas
Hartas, hartas como maiz.

Y allí á versarl., manario,
Y á pelearnos tan bonito,
Y luego á la Tlapisquera
Para dormir calientito

¡Caray, caray, me amolé!
Mejor, mejor nos mataran,
Y no quitarnos así
Así nomás el Tlamapa.

Y luego hasta el refinito
Y toditito licor,
Pos nos va á llevar el diablo,
Nos va á llevar sí patrón

Se emperran en refrescarnos
Como si hiciera calor,
Pos que no ven que el *frijol*
Nos deja tiesos, *siñor?*

Nos quitaron la *cobija*
La cobija de por dentro;
Ya nos tocó la hora mala
Y agua solo beberemos.

Agua aunque sea del Drenaje,
Agua de puros *maclovios*
Que se nos *güelvan* culebras
Y sapos y *tiburonos*.

Pos hora sí estamos *frescos*,
Frescos deveras, caray!
Y hay que aguantarnos manito
Ni modo de repelar.

Salí anoche de las tandas
Del jacalón del Tepache,
Que solo el nombre le queda
Porque no más hay *germanes*.

Tenía una sed de los diablos.
Y estaba sudando....¡tinta!
Y que otro *rimedio?* Así
Un vaso de horchata fría.

CORRIDO DE LA GUERRA

El mundo s' está acabando
es un incendio la tierra;
escuchen con atención
el corrido de la guerra.

Antes veíamos el fuego
muy seguros, desde lejos,
per' ora nos va llegando
la lumbre a los aparejos.

Año fatal del cuarenta,
allá en Uropa el nazismo
desencadenó su juria
produciend' un cataclismo.

Desdi antonces mi han hablado
todititos los qu' encuentro,
de Hítler, el alemán
que lleva el demonio adentro.

Si catrines lu alababan,
el pueblo nu abre la boca
si nu es cuando lo maldice.
y el pueblo no s' equivoca.

Gente leida y escrebida,
dedicada a l' analítica,
dijo qu' es l' aparición
de la bestia apocalítica.

Pa' mi l' endino malora,
a pesar de su raza aria,
vale purita morcilla:
¡Hijo de la china Hilaria!

Aquí lo quisiera ver,
sin tanques y sin aviones,
peliando como pelean
los hombres. no los coyones.

Con mis cuates valedores,
esos que van en la silla,
firmes, como los dorados
de mi jefe Pancho Villa.

Y también con los di a pie,
que todos saben peliar;
estoy siguro que ansí,
no sirve ni pa' empezar.

Cuand' oigo sus amenazas,
m' echo el sombrero de lado
y pienso: "quén dijo miedo,
aquí naiden si ha rajado".

Nu almito gato por liebre
ni por valiente al cobarde;
a Hítler hay que dicirle,
que vaya y güelva a la tarde.

upon the same rich source for the score of *Coronela*, a ballet founded on an incident in a revolutionary ballad.

But it was upon the novel that the corrido of the revolution exerted its most marked influence, for it re-oriented the authors, weaned them from tales of sentiment and society, from European style and theme, and fixed their attention on the woes of the proletariat. Dr. Mariano Azuela (1873) was the first of the post-revolutionary school, and it is interesting to see how his adventurous life supplied him with literary material. After studying medicine in Guadalajara he returned to the place of his birth, Lagos de Moreno. There he married, had a large family, took a modest part in politics, and still found time to write. His first article appeared in 1896 and was followed by several novels exposing the age-old social injustices of Mexico in various of its manifestations. With his philanthropic leanings it was inevitable that he should become a passionate partisan of Francisco I. Madero, who promised to cure all evils. Madero succeeded in forcing Porfirio Díaz' abdication, and in being elected president in his place, but was murdered before he could attempt reforms. General Victoriano Huerta, the leader of the conservatives, then seized power, but Carranza, Obregón and Pancho Villa, feeling the fruits of the revolution would be lost under the new regime, swept down from the north with their men and forced Huerta to resign. Then followed a break between the victorious generals, and Villa retired with his men to Chihuahua. Here he raised his army to forty thousand, much of it cavalry, and armed it with eighty field-pieces he had captured from Huerta.

'CORRIDO DE LA GUERRA'

This modern broadside, dated 1942, continues the tradition into the World War II period, though by that time Mexican broadsides no longer had Posada to give them distinction with his illustrations. The *corrido* commemorates Mexico's breaking of relations with the Axis over the sinking of two Mexican freighters by Nazi submarines. The style of the verses is more in line with what scholars usually think of as the broadside style. On the one hand the writer makes an artificial attempt to reproduce folk speech, mainly by misspelling words; on the other he tries to give elegance to his composition by using 'poetic' devices. There is a vast difference between the style of this broadside and the most pedestrian to come from the Vanegas Arroyo press.

37

XI : *Translation on page 57*

After long preparations, his five troop-trains left Juárez to attack Obregón, entrenched in Celaya.

The first day that Villa threw his forces against Celaya, Obregón beat them off, and I remember Villa's answer when I asked him how things were going. Rather glumly he admitted defeat, and then burst out angrily: 'Pero mañana por la mañana voy a quitarle los pantalones a ese sinverguenza de Obregón' (Tomorrow morning I'll lick the pants off that shameless Obregón!). But he was never even able to cut his suspenders. He did attack the next day, but with the same result. On the last attempt General Obregón threw out a column from the front of Celaya, and Villa saw it break through his center. A peerless guerrilla fighter and a resourceful leader of small bodies of cavalry like his personal guard, called 'Dorados' because they were uniformed in khaki, Villa was untrained in military science and did not know how to maneuver so large an army, and devise its strategy. Instead of commanding the battle from his post of vantage, he hot-headedly jumped on his horse, yelled to his Dorados to follow, and charged the enemy. That was what Obregón had hoped for, and it led to the *coup de grace* that began the rout.

At this time Azuela was an army doctor who lived, fought and suffered with Villa's men on their disastrous retreat northward. He kept copious notes of every incident, and took them wih him when he escaped across the border to El Paso, Texas. He lived a hand-to-mouth existence, often hungry and always penniless, but managed, finally, to whip his notes into a manuscript which he called *Los de abajo*. He tried to sell it, and accepted his best offer of twenty dollars from a Spanish language newspaper, *El Paso del Norte*, published in the city of his exile, where it appeared as a serial in 1915. The next year it came out in a tiny edition and created not even a ripple. A decade later there was a battle among the literary critics as to whether there was a vigorous modern Mexican literature or not. Someone cited *Los de abajo* as the only novel the revolution had produced. There was a rush to reprint it, and Azuela became famous. Since then it has been translated into many languages.

The reason for its success probably lies in Dr. Azuela's ability to strip the Mexican soldier's mind and body of all camouflage, and reveal him, stark and terrible, in his still mediaeval mentality, his insatiable bloodlust, his abysmal Indian cruelty, his magpie-like destructive looting, his orgies of rum and rape, his headlong courage, his cowardice, his stoical acceptance of any fate, his ignorance of why he was fighting and his irrepressible joy in living. It is a series of ruthless, realistic, unforgettable pictures, without the slightest trace of condemnation, defense, or mawkishness.

When he could safely return, Dr. Azuela went to Mexico City and took up his practice of medicine. He did not cease his literary efforts and published other novels in which he told the pitiful tale of the tribulations of middle-class families, during and after the civil war. From these it is apparent that he felt the ideals of the revolution had been betrayed by dishonest politicians who exploited the people as much, if not more than, the 'cientificos' and rich hacendados of the days of Porfirio Díaz.

The chance discovery of *Los de abajo*, ten years after it first appeared, was like the lifting of a sluice gate and released a flood of interpreters of the revolution. The first to follow in Azuela's footsteps was Martín Luis Guzmán (1887). He had seen fighting as a journalist, and, being Chihuahua born, he knew intimately the leaders, Villa, Obregón, Carranza, Angeles and the others, whose personalities he described with fidelity and insight in *El águila y la serpiente* (1928),[1] *La sombra del caudillo* (1929), and a biography of Pancho Villa. Rafael F. Muñoz (1899) added his contribution to the bloody record of the revolution in his tales, *El feroz cabecilla* (1929), *Si me han de matar mañana* (1933), and his novel, *Vámonos con Pancho Villa* (1932).

There were too many contributors to this theme to mention them all, but among them were José Rubén Romero (1890), who used the revolution as a back drop for his costumbrista novels; Nellie Campobello, who in *Cartucho* (1931), told of her childhood spent in the soldier camps of Northern Mexico; and one of the most gifted of all, Gregorio López y Fuentes, whose four novels support the thesis that no matter which party wins, it is the Indian who pays in blood, tears, and suffering.

It is evident from their works that the majority of these writers, like Azuela, suffered the disillusionment that comes after all revolutions, when the reformers, who initiated the movement with high hopes, see it slip into the hands of the selfish opportunists, the sordid politicians who rob and betray the people while mouthing

[1] Translated into English by Harriet de Onis under the title 'The Eagle and the Serpent.' New York, Knopf, 1930.

demagogic clichés. Gradually, this group forsook the recording of the bloody episodes of war to turn their attention to the innumerable problems that followed in its wake.

This new florescense in all the arts, that might be said to have welled up from the very hearts of the people—to have been sung into being by the humble *corrido*—has inspired Mexico's poets, painters, writers and musicians to give new and vigorous life to every expression of her culture, and to make it as autochthonous and deep-rooted in the soil as *tamal* or *tortilla*.

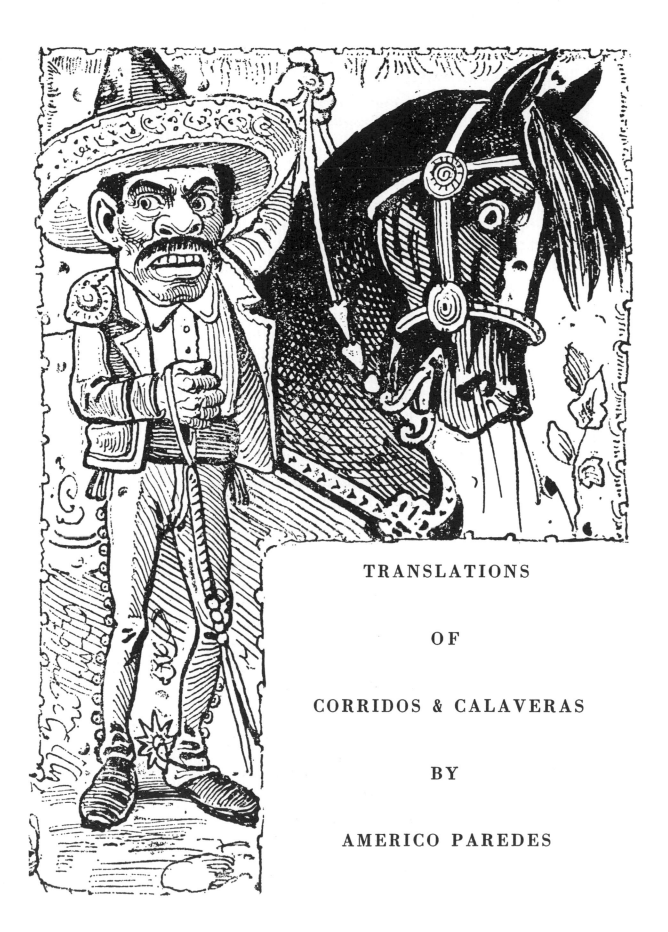

TRANSLATIONS

OF

CORRIDOS & CALAVERAS

BY

AMERICO PAREDES

THE 41 HOMOSEXUALS
Discovered At A Ball On La Paz Street, November 20, 1901.

The Homosexuals Are Here,
So Coquettish And So Dear.

Some very few days ago,
On La Paz, the well-known street,
The gendarmerie were given
A most remarkable treat.

Forty and one of our beaus,
In costume the half of them,
Dressed up like attractive maidens
Danced with vigor and with vim.

And the other half in tails,
Acting the masculine parts,
Took extreme delight in pressing
These famous queers to their hearts.

Dressed up in silk and in satin
To the fashion's latest trick,
Their wigs nicely combed and tidy,
Oh, but they danced with chic!

How elegant were the fans
Which they carried so politely,
And the earrings and the pendants
That swung on their ears so lightly.

Their little faces were painted
With chalk or some other mess—
Lead, powdered rice or ashes—
So you couldn't even guess.

All wearing the finest corsets,
Their feminine curves just so:
Hips, thighs and breasts well rounded—
All artificial, you know.

In short, let us say they looked
Both exciting and alluring,
Dancing away to the rhythm
Of the rattiest of music.

The occasion, it is said,
Was to celebrate with joy
An infamous act, the raffle
Of a fourteen-year-old boy.

Without a care in the world,
And the party at its height,
All the sissies were enjoying
The sweets of that happy night.

When bang! The police have entered,
Catching the queers by surprise!
Now that was something to see:
The hurry, the grief, the cries!

Some try to jump in the privy,
Some try to flee from arrest,
Some are deprived of their senses,
And others are half undressed.

Sound the general alarm!
What uproar! What awful fray!
They weep and squeal, even bark,
But not a one gets away.

The police has them surrounded,
They gather them, one by one;
And straight to the nearest jailhouse
They are taken on the run.

THE BRAVO FROM GUADALAJARA

Take on the Guadalajaran,
You are just wasting his time;
He's not anybody's coward,
Briseño, that is his name.

Don't think I'm from Potosí—
I never backed out or ran;
I come from Santiago district
And I'll take on any man.

Because of my neckerchief
Don't take me for some beginner,
Or if you look at my leggins
Call me ranchero or skinner;
I'll take a shot at the panther,
My hide will not crease agin her;

I have never been afraid,
You know, Tagarno, you sinner;
Even if you're from Zamora
I will have you for my dinner.

My manners are not so ugly,
I will hang on any hook,
And everywhere that I wander
I always launder and cook;
Don't think I'm down from the rancho
Or that I fight in a troupe;
I am looking for the Squirrel
To see who's the biggest rook;
He says he's the Yellow Fever—
I'm going to take a look.

I made a tour of Jalisco
And all of them were my meat;
Alone I shone in 'Canela'
Where I gave them quite a treat;
Well have you seen it, Manuela,
That I'm a man hard to beat;
I found Pancha and Jesús
Playing at love in the street,
He sees me and says, 'Flatiron,
Why don't you put out some heat?'

One life is all that I have,
The same which is bound to leave me;
Don't think that you'll catch me napping,
You'll make a mistake, believe me;
I've never been slow or timid,
I never tremble or start;
You have seen it, Irenea,
The Black One, he doesn't grieve me;
Though I may look like a half-pint
I measure up to the quart.

If the saddle-tree don't suit you,
Jump on and we'll ride it bare;
Here's your servant, Leather Britches,
And don't you think he will scare;
If anyone doesn't like it
Just let him say it out clear;
Isn't it so, pal of mine,
This isn't a basket here?

44

Anyone who wants a mouthful,
Speak up and you get your share.

I'm a famous tapatío
And I have traveled the land
In search of some windy boaster,
I hope there is one around;
In Tepic and in Colima
The finest talent I found,
And even the potosino,
He couldn't make me a stand;
I don't want uncles and cousins:
Here is my club in my hand.

TENDER ENTREATIES

WITH WHICH YOUNG GIRLS FORTY YEARS OF AGE INVOKE
THE MIRACLE-WORKING ST. ANTHONY OF PADUA
PRAYING TO HIM FOR COMFORT

Oh miraculous St. Anthony,
Look on these tears which I wipe,
I pray you give me a husband
Because I am overripe.

St. Anthony beatific,
Oh Saint of my fervent prayer,
Give me, for pity, a husband
And release me from this care;
Aged, one-armed, paralytic,
Either with or without his hair,
Just as long as he will have me—
A soldier of any type;
All I want is to get married
Because I am overripe!

I do not ask for a general,
A marquis, count, or a duke;
All that I want is a man
Who'll give me a second look;

I don't care if he's a robber
Or some other kind of crook,
Do you not see how I suffer
In the cruel, maternal gripe?
A husband, oh dear St. Anthony,
Because I am overripe!

Most compassionate of saints,
I ask you with hope devout
That you will give me a mate,
No matter the shame or doubt;
If there is no other way
An old man, perhaps, with gout,
Since the others run so fast;
Oh, Saint, please get me a fellow!
Have pity on this poor woman,
Because I am more than mellow!

To your charity and power
Oh St. Anthony I pray,
Give me at least an old widower
Who will make me rich some day;
Have pity on me, I beg you,
And do no longer delay;
I'll be married to the Devil,
A scoundrel of any stripe—
Please arrange my matrimony
Because I am overripe!

VERY EXTRAVAGANT VERSES

BOTH FABULOUS AND AMUSING

To laugh And To Pass The Time,
A Special Treat For The Curious.

A Coyote made his entrance
Into León, the famous city,
When he was stopped by a Buzzard
Who was patrolman on duty.

Told him right out on the street,
'Say friend, I would like to know
Where do you think you are going with
That married woman in tow?'

He took him off to the judge
Around the corner pell-mell;
This last was a handsome Bobcat
That in a kitchen did dwell;
A little Swallow, poor soul,
On being told what befell
To the plaza from her nest
She flew at a rapid rate
In search of a Turtle Dove
For she had no legal mate.

From the city of Commotion
The evening of that same day
A Screech Owl also arrived
On discovering the way;
To have a word with Coyote
The Fox then made his essay
When on horseback, at a trot,
Came a Coon of great renown,
Who made a terrible mess
Of all the girls in the town.

One barefoot, one with a sandal,
There came in another pair:
Mrs. Squirrel and Mr. Possum
With the children in their care,
And all the crowd laughed and jested
To see that they had no hair;
A Mosquito and a Scorpion,
Thinking nobody had seen them,
Went off to the marketplace
To eat a melon between them.

All this time a Fish was writing
With no small amount of care
What an Eagle was dictating,
While seated upon a chair,
A White Rabbit was the table;
And everyone was amazed
To see a Fly and a Rat
Coming in out of the street,

All dressed up in silver braid
From their heads down to their feet.

'There isn't the slightest doubt
That everything has its trick,'
So did the Tortoise remark
To the Spider and the Tick.
'Let us go with Friend Coyote,
We can leave at dawn tomorrow.'
Then the Hornet had his say,
'I have always been a rover;
I will go along with you;
Just wait till the year is over.'

'How long is a mere twelve months?'
A big drunken Weevil said.
'Let us cease this foolish talk
And have a few drinks instead.'
And about that time a Mule
Arrived on his Parrot steed,
And a Lizard then inquired,
'What's up, my long-legged pet?
If God will be good to me
I'll marry your daughter yet.'

.   .   .   .
.   .   .   .

At the last a speedy Hare
Came to join them in their cups,
A Doe that was wearing chaps,
And a little Bitch with pups;
They looked about and they saw
How many had joined the fun,
So they went off to a fiesta,
There stayed not a single one;
And dancing to the 'Mascota'
They passed the center of León.

DEATH'S-HEADS ARE SOLD BY THE TON

All At The Price Of A Dime
The Whole Of Mexico City
HAS SEEN NOTHING OF THE KIND

This is a most truthful saw,
As anyone will agree:
He who has never been born
A death's-head will never be.

For the amusement of mortals
We have concocted this salad;
Even the soldier may shudder
On the reading of this ballad.

Death's-head is the Englishman,
A skull-and-bones, Si Señor;
And the Frenchman is a death's-head,
And Faure and Sadi Carnot;
Chinese, American, Pope,
And the Cardinals also;
The Kings, the Dukes and Advisors,
And even the Chief of State,
In the grace they all are equal:
Here are death's-heads by the crate.

The general is a death's-head,
And all of his aides as well,
The colonels and the commanders
And the captain with his bile;
The subalterns in their turn
Will be death's-heads in a while;
The same will happen to sergeants,
To the corporals in files,
And to the soldiers by hundreds:
Here are your death's-heads in piles.

And all the dishonest merchants
Will end up as grinning skulls,
This time it will really happen,
And all the owners of stalls,
The actors with their pretending
They're better than anyone,
The owners of cheques and monies,
Their fortunate days are done:

All bones, half-eaten and rotten,
Here are death's-heads by the ton.

Death's-head is also the tumbler
With the circus now in town,
Death's-head is the tavern keeper
And death's-head also the clown;
The druggist, the pawn-shop owner,
The bigots who pray and weep,
And every rascally vender
Who says that his goods are cheap,
All those who deceive the public:
Here are death's-heads in a heap.

THE AMERICAN MOSQUITO

The American mosquito
Has just arrived, so they say;
To this, our Mexican soil,
He's come for a holiday.

Sunday they say he embarked,
Through Laredo he appears,
He goes as far as Saltillo
Stinging everybody's ears;
And the women at the station,
He made them travel, the dears;
Why he even made them sweat,
That inhuman little critter;
And soon everyone was shouting:
'The American mosquito!'

Next he went to Guanajuato
Where he really played the clown;
He visited in Marfil
Though he didn't see the town;
He was mischievous and haughty
And made many people frown;
He finally stung the backside
Of a military leader;
He is very, very rude:
The American mosquito.

He took Irapuato road
And through Pénjamo he cast,
And then retracing his footsteps
Reached Uriangato at last;
The Hacienda Villachato
Was ruins after he passed,
The people were in a panic;
Though there was no one to heed her,
Still old Emeteria shouted:
'The American mosquito!'

Piedra Gorda, La Sandía,
And then to San Juan—the gate;
'What a fearsome beast! My Heavens!'
Said an old woman of late.
Tell me, my dear don Pascual,
Have you been mosquito bait?
He's so pitiless and tiny,
And could anything be neater?
Can you tell me what he says,
The American mosquito?

VERSES OF VALENTIN MANCERA

Brought From The State Of Guanajuato
IN EIGHTEEN HUNDRED AND EIGHTY
WELL I REMEMBER THE DAY
THEY KILLED
VALENTIN MANCERA
The Bravest Among The Brave

Terrible woe
He carries within his heart!
No one to show him pity,
No one to take his part.
            (Repeat after each quatrain.)

It was the Nineteenth of March,
At four o'clock in the morning,
When the treacherous San Juana
Went out to do her informing.

51

'Very good morning, Señor,
Don Dionisio Catalán;
I have a jewel for you
That you have sought in San Juan.'

They went eagerly to get him,
The men who took him were four;
So Don Dionisio could see him,
They led him straight to his door.

To the tune of a guitar
Some special music they played him
On the agonies of death,
Because San Juana betrayed him.

So poor Valentín Mancera,
Fate dealt him a losing hand;
For a firing squad has shot him
By the government's command.

Then his poor mother replied,
'Señores, I beg permission
That this Valentín Mancera
Will not die without confession.'

'Let no such favor be done,'
All of the Spaniards protested.
'We're scared to death of Mancera,
Who is by us much detested.'

Oh, what a fate was Mancera's,
And who would have ever guessed
That a firing squad would shoot him,
And without having confessed.

Now this Valentín Mancera
Was not very big or tall;
They say he was pretty slender,
They say he was pretty small.

From Mexico came the word
The Government wanted him,
And the President remarked,
'I'm sorry for Valentín.'

All the Spanish gachupines
Dressed up in their Sunday best,
And they went to 'El Vapor'
And drank to Mancera's death.

52

And now I must say farewell,
With all the angels in flight;
They killed Valentín Mancera,
Who gave the Spaniards a fright.

. . . .
. . . .

GENUINE VERSES ABOUT LINO ZAMORA

Brought From The Mining Town of Zacatecas

Alas for Lino Zamora,
That his fate should be so cruel!
In the town of Zacatecas
He has been killed by a bull.

Rose, little rose, flower of thyme,
There won't be another like him,
Not until the end of time.

When he left from Guanajuato
Four times did they hear him sigh,
While crossing Cerro Trozado,
His heart told him he would die.

Rose, little rose, flower of Spain,
Lino Zamora is dead,
Prisciliana is to blame.....

To Jerez, to sign a contract,
Lino sent Braulio away;
Till the contract was completed
In that Jerez he must stay.

Rose, little rose, flower of snow,
Lino Zamora is dead,
He must have wanted it so.

He returned on Thursday morning
From Jerez, where he had been.
'Prisciliana is with Lino,'
Then said his brother, Martín.

Rose, little rose, rose of the lake,
Lino Zamora is dead
Because he made a mistake.

On Thursday, August the Fourteenth,
The afternoon of the day,
The best swordsman in the country
Had already passed away.

He came to Tacuba street,
Where Lino Zamora stood,
'Here is where I must kill you
And let you lie in your blood.'

Rose, little rose, flower of green,
Lino Zamora is dead,
He will nevermore be seen.

.   .   .   .

.   .   .   .

And bitterly did she weep,
The mother that gave him birth,
To see her beloved Lino
Being put into the earth.

Rose, little rose, flower of green,
Once you have buried Zamora
He will nevermore be seen.

And how bitter were the tears
Of all his cuadrilla *brave,*
To see that their matador
Was being put in the grave.

Rose, little rose, flower so red,
For his first banderillero
With one bullet shot him dead.

And with this I say farewell,
In the rays of the Aurora;
This is the end of the singing
In memory of Zamora.

Rose, little rose, rose again,
Lino Zamora is dead;
Requiescat in pace, Amén.

SAD AND AMUSING LEAVE-TAKING
OF THE CATHEDRAL CLOCK
OF MEXICO

The old clock in the Cathedral
Has come to his final hour,
And he says his last goodnight
Perched on the top of his tower.

Now the poor ancient one goes
After a long, useful life;
And he takes with him much history,
Pages of glory and strife.

Farewell Mexico! The progress
Of this your capital city
Is the reason that you must
Put me away without pity;
I am old, and like some evil
You choose to cast me aside;
I find that I have been sentenced
All covered with soot to lie,
And far away from the crowds
In a corner I must die.

Flagpole which rested upon me,
A final farewell, goodnight;
It was on you that it fluttered—
Always towering and bright—
The flag of our native soil,
Amid whose beautiful flight
History came to recover
Events that are past belief:
Gigantic pages of glory
And the bitter tears of grief.

Of the war for Independence
I witnessed the struggle brief;
Then came a treacherous power
Raising its standard—the cock;
The field of the Fifth of May
Made him the shame of the flock:
We left him featherless, cackling,
No longer proud of his power;
Because this is not the soil
For the vassal's seed to flower.

Farewell, oh beloved bells,
Within those towers, my neighbors;
To answer your crystal notes
Was one of my sweetest labors;
Beloved sisters, adieu,
The years are my overthrow;
They have cast me out forever
To lament an exile's woe;
Toll for me, for I am going
Where all the dead bodies go.

LAMENTATIONS OF A DRUNK

Over The Closing Of Saloons And Pulque Shops

The Devil may take us now!
I am done! I'm really sunk!
After twelve o'clock on Sunday
I'm forbidden to get drunk.

All the pulque shops will close,
And the cantinas as well;
And so to water we're driven
Like oxen, our thirst to quell.

And me, who with my guitar
Would go on a Sunday morn
To down a couple of measures
As big as bushels of corn.

And after some versifying
Would follow a little fight;
Then to jail with all my buddies
For a warm and pleasant night.

Damn! But they fixed us good!
It would be better to kill us
Than to take from us this way
The nectar that used to fill us.

The fine tequila, the brandy,
And all other kinds of liquor;
The Devil take us, Señor,
They sure could have killed us quicker.

They want us to freshen up,
As if it were summer. Lord!
When the frijoles we eat
Leave us as stiff as a board.

They took our covers away,
Those that covered us within;
And now we must take to water
And shiver inside our skin.

And water it then must be,
No matter how foul or smelly;
We'll be breeding toads and snakes
And even sharks in our belly.

So now we are fresh enough,
As fresh as the morning dew;
You must learn to bear it, brother;
There is nothing we can do.

At the Tepache pavilion,
As I was leaving the same—
It's the haunt of thieves and robbers
Though it keeps its early fame—

I was sweating like the Devil
And so thirsty that I neighed;
So what could I do but order . . .
A glass of cold lemonade!

THE CORRIDO OF THE WAR

The world is about to end,
The whole earth is catching fire;
Come and listen with attention
To the ballad of the war.

We used to sit back and watch,
Secure from the distant battle;
Now the flames are burning us
At the edges of the saddle.

Nineteen-forty, fateful year,
The Germans and their Nazism
Unleashed their fury in Europe,
Producing a cataclysm.

Ever since then I've been told,
When I talk to men or women,
All about Hitler, the German
Who is possessed by a demon.

If some of the dudes have praised him,
No comment the people make,
Except if it is to curse him;
The people make no mistake.

And those who can read and write,
Whose thinking is analytic,
Say that Hitler is the beast
Mentioned in the Apocalyptic.

In spite of his Aryan race
He is no elegant critter;
He's nothing but sausage meat,
He's just a son of a . . . bitter.

I'd like to have him right here,
Without a plane or a tank,
To see if he's really brave
Or just a cowardly skunk.

With all my faithful companions,
Those that can fight in the saddle,
Like the troops of Pancho Villa
We will go join in the battle.

And also the ones on foot,
They also would like to go;
I bet Hitler and his men
Will scarcely give us a show.

When I hear of Hitler's threats,
I put my hat on my ear
And think, 'What have we to lose?
No one is a coward here.'

Don't tell me the moon is cheese,
Nor give me catmeat for hare;
And what we must say to Hitler
Is to go . . . and tell him where.

BIBLIOGRAPHY

Probably the three most informative books on the *Corrido* are as follows:

El Romance Español y el Corrido Mexicano por Vicente T. Mendoza, Ediciones de la Universidad Autónoma, Mexico, 1939.

La Décima en Mexico, Glosas y Valonas, por Vicente T. Mendoza, Instituto Nacional de la Tradición, Buenos Aires, Argentina, 1947.

The Mexican Corrido as a Source for Interpretive Study of Modern Mexico (1870–1950) by Merle E. Simmons, Indiana University Publications, Humanity Series No. 38, Indiana University Press, Bloomington, 1957.

*The corridos and calaveras reproduced here are from a collection
made by the author in Mexico, and now belonging to
The Hall of the Horsemen of the Americas*
THE UNIVERSITY OF TEXAS
*1,000 copies of this second printing have been printed and bound by
The Printing Division of The University of Texas
Design by Kim Taylor*